How to SELL

A Pen - *Really*

Seduce Your Audience into

Anything Using Sales Psychology

PAUL DEMOCRITOU

Copyright © 2018 by Paul Democritou and Sandra Seymour

All rights reserved. This book or any portion thereof may not be reproduced or used in any manner whatsoever without the express written permission of the publisher except for the use of brief quotations in a book review.

First Printing, 2018
ISBN 9781728685182

Paul Democritou
Athens, Greece

http://SellAPen.com

Although the author and publisher have made every effort to ensure that the information in this book was correct at press time, the author and publisher do not assume and hereby disclaim any liability to any party for any loss, damage, or disruption caused by errors or omissions, whether such errors or omissions result from negligence, accident, or any other cause.

Cover design by Rob Williams (Ilovemycover.com)
Book design and editing by Sandra Seymour

For Helen,
Cancer may have taken you, but you will be forever in my heart.

Dino and George,
I am proud to call you my nephews

Mother,
Keep fighting, you can beat it.

Contents

Foreword 1
Introduction 5
3 Reasons You Suck at Sales 11
7 Daily Habits for Sales Success 16
Get Your Audience's A-List Attention 27
Serve a Niche, Solve a Problem 30
Who's on Your List? 34
Build Your Own Sales Funnel 37
How to Sell on the Phone 42
How to Meet and Greet 47
The Trump Handshake 53
How to Make People Like You 57
How to sell anyone anything 64
Anchoring 75
How to persuade anyone 78
Closing Objections 86
I Want to Think About It 97
Three Great Closes 101
Referrals 108
Putting it all together 111
Now, Sell Me A Pen 116
About the Author 118
Also by Paul Democritou 119
Bibliography 121

Foreword

Have you ever noticed sometimes you meet someone, and quickly feel as though you have known them for years? How some people light up the room with their presence, and some can convince you to do anything, their enthusiasm is so infectious?

Then there are those who are so alive, so active, and ambitious in their every plan, you can't help following them, just to see what they'll do next?

Paul Democritou is all those things, and more.

When we first met online, he was a fan of my *The Closers* series, and a student of sales science. He was struggling financially after the Greek crisis hit his family hard and reached out to me for advice.

I told him the same thing I tell everyone in his position; "Go back to basics. Rebuild. If you've done it before, you can do it again."

Unlike most, Paul listened. And over the next few years, he pieced his finances back together.

Then, in 2016, tragedy struck. Paul was diagnosed with cancer. He had aggressive Non-

Hodgkin's Lymphoma and was advised to embark on a six-month course of treatment, including chemotherapy, followed by a bone marrow transplant to save his life.

He could have been forgiven at that point for retreating, focusing on the treatment, and waiting until he recovered to rebuild yet again.

Not Paul.

Paul wrote a book while fighting cancer.

He started a YouTube channel, and started teaching everything he knew about sales and success.

He wrote, and he hustled. And when the treatment got too much, he dictated sections of his manuscript and had them transcribed.

When he asked me to write the foreword to that first book, *Success!* he didn't have to ask twice. And when Paul said he would love to write a book with me one day, I had no hesitation.

It was my pleasure to work with Paul on *The Closers – Part 3*, a book so long overdue I had begun to think it might never be written.

The one thing I didn't want *The Closers - Part 3* to be was "Son of the Closers," a rehashing of old content. I wanted it to be new and different, yet still touch on those things that make sales and closing work.

In the end *The Closers - Part 3* was much more than a simple rehashing of my previous works. Paul brought fresh insight, and a breadth and depth of knowledge of modern sales technology that taught me a thing or two along the way.

FOREWORD

Who says you can't teach an old dog new tricks?

I have been in sales over fifty years. I rubbed shoulders with some of the greatest salesmen of the twentieth century, from Zig Ziglar to Napoleon Hill.

Doctor Hill mentored me in my early career during the last three years of his life. He taught me first-hand how to apply his theory in practice. I was proud to be his last protégé.

Fortunately, I've been able to work with Paul for more than three years now, and plan to continue to do so for quite some time.

I have mentored many people over the years, but Paul has been and remains one of my best students, and I am proud to pass the baton to him. A long and fine tradition of salesmanship and sales training is safe in his hands.

I firmly believe Paul Democritou will be one of the greats of the twenty-first century, continuing a proud tradition.

Ben Gay III
Placerville, CA
06 September 2018
TheLastProtege.com
WWW.BFG3.COM

Introduction

Four words strike fear into the hearts of would-be salespeople every day. "Sell me this pen."

I blame Hollywood.

At the end of the movie *The Wolf of Wall Street*, Jordan Belfort, played by Leonardo DiCaprio, asks a room of people to sell him a pen.

It has since become an even more common interview question for sales positions, designed to put the salesperson on the spot and test their understanding of the sales process.

If you stick around in sales long enough, and you haven't already heard this challenge, you will.

But don't worry, I've got your back.

Even if you're a complete novice, have never held a sales position before, and have no idea where to start, by following the steps laid out in this book you will learn everything you need to know about sales to become a top salesperson with any company.

But how, when it's so slim?

Because there's no fluff, no filler. Everything is distilled down to its essence and laid out in Plain English.

I want to make learning sales so simple, an eight-year-old can do it. I want you to carry this book with you always. When a deal goes South, I want you to read through it, and pinpoint where you went wrong. Do that enough times, and you won't go wrong any more.

So, how do you sell a pen?

The first thing to understand is that it's a trick question.

Most salespeople will try and sell you the pen and the benefits. Much like the actors in the final scene of the film, they'll say things like:

"It's an amazing pen, for professionals,"

"It's a nice pen. You can use the pen to write down thoughts from your life, so you can remember,"

"This pen works, and I personally love this pen."

All that does is tell the interviewer you don't understand the sales process.

You're not a salesperson.

You're not supposed to do that. That was the point. The idea is to use the "sell a pen," prompt to walk the interviewer through your sales process.

It's also an effective way to teach sales.

Which is how this book came about.

INTRODUCTION

One of my most popular YouTube videos is a tongue-in-cheek pen sales pitch that demonstrates the sales process.

You will find it and other sales training videos at https://www.youtube.com/pauldemocritou.

One day, my editor and I were discussing my publishing strategy. I had already published *Success! Improvise, Adapt, Overcome* and co-written *The Closers - Part 3* with living legend Ben Gay III. I had another co-authored book, about succeeding with cryptocurrency with Blaise Mathai, and one of Success Interviews with people who are successful in their field in the pipeline.

I needed a book that offered the sales success essentials as an entry point for new salespeople, that would also serve as a prompt for more seasoned professionals. Something that I could give new recruits as a primer, but that would have value for anyone in need of a refresher course.

Since I was travelling a lot between Poland, Greece, and Bulgaria advising cryptocurrency start-ups Experty and Evido on market growth, sales, and marketing, my time to create new content for the book was limited.

It looked as though the essentials book would have to wait. Prepared to table the idea for a while, we started talking about the sales training videos on my YouTube channel.

Before long, we realised that between the channel videos, and a few excerpts from the other books, most of the content for the book already existed; it just needed to be transcribed, organized, and edited.

Which meant, apart from a few phone calls and galley proofing, most of my work was already done.

Don't you just love it when that happens?

I know I do.

My editor was less thrilled, since I also wanted to sneak this book into the publishing schedule before the two *Success!* books, and still get them all out before the end of the year.

That meant burning the midnight oil, and rescheduling. But she's a champ like that, I assured myself, and all three books would no doubt be ready in time, while I could focus on other things.

Even better, the video *How To Sell a Pen, Really* had started ranking for a few high-traffic keywords and attracting views on YouTube. It was gaining traction. Wouldn't it be cool, we spit-balled, if we could somehow capitalize on that, and turn it into a brand?

First, we domain checked, and discovered that while so many long tail versions of the phase "Sell me this pen," were registered already, the short form, "Sell a pen," was available. I registered it and threw up an email registration page.

Then she hit me with it.

"I'll fit the book in," she said, "but if we're doing this, it's not just going to be a book."

Since we'd been talking about putting an online course together for a while, I assumed that was what she meant.

Introduction

I was only half right.

Over the next few minutes, my editor outlined a vision. Of a book that connected the YouTube channel and social media accounts to a website. Of a book, and associated training course. And so much more. A brand.

But driving people from social media to a website had become increasingly tough. For one thing, the platforms don't want you to send traffic elsewhere, they want eyeballs on their site, not yours.

We considered giving something away as a lead magnet. But lead magnets tend to attract freebie seekers. People who collect free downloads, and never get around to reading them, let alone implementing their ideas.

After all no one takes free advice.

We didn't want a huge list full of freebie hunters. That's like holding onto a massive sack of wind.

We wanted a smaller list, full of action-takers. People who wanted to learn, and then implement what they learned.

What better way than a competition?

Now, I'll explain the competition we came up with at the end of the book. Because, of course, as an action-taker, you're going to want to enter.

But before you enter, you need to read the book.

So, no skipping ahead.

Read the book first.

Then go to SellAPen.com and enter the competition.

Deal?

Promise?

Good.

3 Reasons You Suck at Sales

Just to be clear, there are potentially more than three reasons you might suck at sales. You might have bad breath. You might have poor personal hygiene, or no sense of personal space.

But I'm in several social media groups online where salespeople talk about sales. Some of the things they say drive me crazy. These are the three biggest issues I see daily, that are so easy to correct, you'd be an idiot not to deal with them up front.

Those who can't sell, teach

If you believe this, then you either think you know it all, or you're an idiot.

Hear me out.

Teaching is an art. Not everyone can do it effectively. I could just as easily turn that around, and say, "Those who can't teach, sell."

Some of the best sports coaches in the world, whether it's soccer, basketball, or any other sport, don't play. They coach.

I could go on, but the bottom line is, if you believe this, you're probably suffering from the Dunning-Kruger Effect.

There are four stages to learning any skill:

- Unconscious Incompetence – You've never done it, but it looks easy
- Conscious Incompetence – You try, and it's not as easy as it looks.
- Conscious Competence – You have practiced and can do it with concentrated effort.
- Unconscious Competence – You have done it so often, you can do it without paying attention.

The Dunning-Kreuger Effect (Kruger & Dunning, Dec 1999) says that

> *Across 4 studies, the authors found that participants scoring in the bottom quartile on tests of humor, grammar, and logic grossly overestimated their test performance and ability. Although their test scores put them in the 12th percentile, they estimated themselves to be in the 62nd. Several analyses linked this miscalibration to deficits in metacognitive skill, or the capacity to distinguish accuracy from error.*

This is a cognitive bias (an error in thinking) of illusory superiority.

Translation?

Idiots don't know they're idiots.

Fools are overconfident, while experts often doubt themselves.

So, when you find yourself stubbornly defending your opinion as fact, or arguing with someone, stop and question your confidence.

Is it possible you could be mistaken?

Is it possible you could learn something from this person?

Even if you're right and they're wrong, it never hurts to listen to another opinion, or consider a different point of view.

Don't climb Mount Stupid.

You think you know it all

Not surprising then, the second reason you suck at sales is that you think you know it all.

We all know about the ABC of sales, "**A**lways **B**e **C**losing."

But you need to always be learning.

Sales experts learn from everyone and everything. We learn from coaches, managers, kids, mentors, books, videos, podcasts. You name it, we are constantly learning from it.

With the attitude that those who can't sell teach, you're not selling, you're not learning. You're limiting yourself.

Get over it. Get over your ego and always be learning.

It doesn't matter who your manager is, there's something you can learn from them. Even if he sucks at sales, there is something to learn.

Commit to learning something from everyone.

As French Scientist Claude Bernard (1813-1878) said, "It is what we already know that often prevents us from learning."

You have a lousy attitude

If you're not learning because you think you know it all already, you have a lousy attitude.

In a social media group, I saw a salesperson complaining that a customer was wasting his time. He posted the messages that were going back and forth between him and the customer. I read them, and the salesperson had made some vital mistakes.

But if you asked him, he probably wouldn't agree.

As I scrolled down, most of the comments from the group were on the side of the salesperson, in complete denial.

One even commented, "I hate window shoppers. Tell him to go…"

I'll let you imagine your own ending to that, but it wasn't repeatable.

Such a disgusting attitude.

A mentality like that might get you a few loose teeth, but it won't get you any sales.

It's small-minded and spiteful. It has no clue how to win customers over, and no clue what win-win is. With an attitude like that, you don't know how to sell.

Because you think you know it all and aren't learning, you will never know how to sell, and will never make it in the field.

The best thing you can do is leave.

Stop trying to sell and go work somewhere else. Preferably somewhere you don't have to work with other people.

Or, open your mind, realise you still have something to learn, and keep reading. We might make a salesperson out of you yet.

7 Daily Habits for Sales Success

Most people don't realise that sales is a sport. Just like any sport, it's vital to increase your skills to improve.

What are the seven habits of highly successful salespeople, and how can you use this information to get more sales?

Vision your day the night before

Have you ever had a feeling something was going to happen, and it did? Maybe you bet on red at the roulette table and just knew it was going to pay off.

You can consciously create that feeling of positive anticipation in your daily life with one simple habit.

Vision your day the night before and envision the sale before the close.

Spend a few minutes every evening running through the next day's To Dos, appointments, goals, and activities in your head, and imagining them turning out well.

This will define your mindset. You will wake up with a mission, with a purpose, with a goal.

There are two things at play here.

First, much like the Dunning-Kreuger effect, where we overestimate our intellectual abilities, research from the Kellogg School (The power of temptation, 2009) highlights a cognitive "restraint bias."

This says we overestimate our ability to focus and resist temptation in the future. We justify procrastinating with the flawed belief that we will have more will power later.

And those with the least willpower are most likely to overestimate their ability to focus.

Second, the power of envisioning yourself doing something to improve your results is now scientifically supported. It's no longer solely the province of New Age Thinkers and Motivational Speakers.

Multiple medical studies have used fMRI scan images to study activity in the brain in real time. They have repeatedly found that thinking about an activity without doing it lights up the same areas in the brain as actually doing it.

And multiple studies measuring muscle gain in groups of subjects who either performed an exercise, or only visualised it found that while those performing the exercises gained more muscle mass, even participants who only imagined exercising were able to build muscle.

This is real, people. Any bodybuilder or power lifter can tell you this. I used to do it in gym!

You can THINK yourself better at ANYTHING.

Smile

Smile every day, when you get up, before you go to work. If you smile every day, smiling will become a habit. It will become a part of your character, and you will be a more positive person.

This helps in life, in sales, in everything.

Smiling even when you don't feel like it will help improve your mood, too. Even a fake smile, held for seven to twelve seconds can lift your spirits.

That's because body language doesn't just reflect your mood, it creates it. Change your posture, change your mood.

Neurologist Dr. Isha Gupta says smiling releases chemicals in the brain, that make us happy (NBC News, 2017)

"Dopamine increases our feelings of happiness. Serotonin release is associated with reduced stress. Low levels of serotonin are associated with depression and aggression," says Dr. Gupta. "Low levels of dopamine are also associated with depression."

This doesn't just work in the moment, either. Your character is a combination of your habits combined. Smiling now just make you happier now, it makes you happier long-term.

Listening

If you listen to your customer carefully, they will tell you what they want or what they want to hear.

This also helps build rapport, and helps people to know, like, and trust you, and it works the same with your personal relationships.

When I first started listening to living legend Ben Gay III and we talked on the phone, every time I spoke, he would stop in silence, and listen. I noticed that this grabbed my attention, but I also wanted to listen to him more.

When I started doing this, just stopping talking and listening when the other person spoke (even if I was half-way through a sentence) I soon noticed that people started to respect me more, and it increased my sales.

Peter Bregman, author of *Four Seconds: All the Time You Need to Stop Counter-Productive Habits and Get the Results You Want* says (Bregman, 2015) "listening is far more persuasive than speaking."

In in a Psychology Today article, *If You Want People to Listen, Stop Talking* he describes how one managing director at a financial services firm developed "an uncanny ability to move a roomful of people to his perspective."

His secret? Listening, and allowing other people to step into the silence.

Then, once he had heard everyone's point of view, feeding it back to them, so that they felt heard.

Only then would he put forth an opinion, which, though often unpopular, would most often be accepted by everyone as the wisest in the room.

Always be learning

I said it before and I will say it again. Always be learning. Keep an open mind and commit to learning something new every day.

Go to seminars. Read books. Attend webinars. Listen to podcasts, watch videos.

You don't know everything. Even if you did, without reinforcement, you will forget. That's what Continuous Professional Development is all about.

You have to keep learning and practicing your art to stay ahead of the game.

Study sales and learn something that makes you better every single day.

Study psychology, body language, rhetoric.

Suggested reading:

- *The Magic of Thinking Big* - David Schwartz
- *Contagious* - Jonah Berger
- *Tube Ritual Volume 1* - Brian G Johnson
- *The Closers - Part 3* - Ben Gay III & Paul Democritou
- *Success! Improvise, Adapt, Overcome* - Paul Democritou
- *How to Win Friends & Influence People* - Dale Carnegie
- *How to Fail at Almost Everything & Still Win Big* - Scott Adams
- *48 Laws of Power* - Robert Greene
- *The Definitive Art of Body Language* - Allan & Barbara Pease
- *Never Split the Difference* - Chris Voss
- *The 10X Rule* - Grant Cardone

For an updated reading list visit my website at http://pauldemocritou.com/resources.

Leave it on the coat hangar

Leave your problems outside the office. I literally hang a coat hanger outside the room, where people see it before they come in. It's there to remind them to hang up their problems and leave them outside.

I don't care if you had a fight with your spouse, spilled your morning coffee, stubbed your toe, or got caught up in traffic. That's all in the past. Leave your negativity outside the office.

One effective way to get a negative experience out of your head is to reframe it. Run through it one time in your imagination, but imagine it ending differently. Think of one thing you could have done differently to achieve a better outcome, learn from it, and let it go.

This "counterfactual thinking" can be good for you. It's how you learn from your mistakes.

But make sure the details you change are things you could have said or done, not things other people could have said or done, or unchangeable background events.

If you can't think of how things could have gone better, try and imagine a way they could have been worse, and be grateful they weren't.

For example, if you had a fight with your spouse, you might think, "I could have phrased that better."

If you stubbed your toe, you might think, "I could have been looking where I was going, instead of reading my email on my phone."

If you were stuck in traffic, you might think, "At least I wasn't in a crash, and didn't get hurt."

Even if it's important to you, most people don't care. Your clients don't care. The people you speak to on the phone don't care.

Even the people who do care can't change it for you. You have to do that for yourself, by changing your thoughts.

Leave your problems outside the door, focus on your work, and get those deals. You may be surprised to find some of those problems have wandered off when you go to collect them on the way home.

Buy a pair of scissors

You can 10X your sales by buying a pair of Scissors!

Back when networking meant meeting people and swapping business cards, when I swapped cards, I would note on the back their hobbies, interests, or anything else I knew about them.

Then, whenever I read a magazine, I would look at the articles, and if they were of interest to any of my contacts, I would cut them out and send them to the people I thought would be interested.

Today, you don't even need to use a pair of scissors, or post anything.

You can just take a snapshot using your cell phone, and send it to them by email or messenger, or whatever their preferred communication method is. Or you can tag people in social media who might be interested in a post or article.

How is this different than just sharing posts, or retweeting something you've seen?

When you tag someone, they know you're thinking about them specifically. They appreciate you remembering what they like, and it starts to build a relationship beyond just trying to sell them your latest product or offer.

This taps into the cognitive bias of reciprocity. Reciprocity bias refers to the impulse to treat people the way they treat us.

In a positive light, people feel the need to return favours. If you invite someone to your birthday party, they feel obliged to invite you to theirs. If someone gives you a Christmas present, you feel obliged to give them something in return. In fact, you often feel the need to get them something on the same scale or even better.

In a negative light, it also explains the revenge impulse, and tit-for-tat retaliation in petty squabbles.

How do you use this in sales?

In his book *Influence*, Robert Cialdini describes how one Indian supermarket sold a thousand pounds of cheese in a few hours, by inviting customers to cut off their own slices as free samples. Because they were inclined to be more generous in their free sample sizes, they also felt obliged to buy more.

A simple way is to host an annual event and invite all your clients. They see you as a great guy, you have chance to network, and collect referrals, set appointments, close deals, and increase customer loyalty all in one go.

A lot of people think networking is going out and meeting new people. Networking is also going out with people you already know and past clients.

It's building those relationships. It's much easier to re-sell an existing client, than to sell a new client. Network with people you already know, not only people you just met.

People you already know are hot leads. They already know you. If you have learned to be likeable, they will like and trust you. You know a lot about them, and they feel safer.

It also taps into the "recency bias," which explains why people give more weight to recent events in decision making than to events that happened longer ago. This incidentally is why the last act is often the judged more favourably in talent shows; it's the one that's freshest in the audience's minds.

Simply staying in regular contact, and making your communication personal, increases your chances of getting a sale when your contact needs something you can provide.

This is why advertisers talk about running constant advertising to keep a brand "top of mind."

Practice speaking online and offline

Practice giving your presentation, your elevator speech, or a three-minute speech on your favourite subject in front of the mirror every day.

It doesn't matter if your speech is scripted, and the same every day, or if you improvise, at least to start with.

I use a video camera. It allows me to play my speech back and watch it more critically.

You can even post your daily practice to YouTube! Make a video diary and put it in one video one day!

Why practice public speaking?

You need to be confident and competent when speaking to contacts both online and offline. This includes on social media, in emails, and on speaking engagements and sales presentations.

Speaking online using social media also has the added benefit of filling your pipeline. Speaking offline even for free, will increase your net worth.

But there's more to it than that.

According to Toastmasters, "Public speaking is listed as American's number-one fear, before death at number five, and loneliness, weighing in at number seven."

Most people are more afraid of speaking in public than of dying.

That's sad.

So, that's one reason to practice public speaking. Because the more you do something, the less scary it feels.

According to psychologist Josh King (King, n.d.), practicing any new skill in a low-stress environment has three major benefits:

- You improve the skill itself, which increases your chances of doing it well when it counts
- You replace old habits with new ones
- You strengthen your habit self-improvement

In other words, practicing any new skill doesn't just increase your performance in that skill. It helps replace old bad habits and it makes you more likely to learn other new skills and replace other bad habits in the future.

Get Your Audience's A-List Attention

In *The Art of War*, Sun Tsu says, "Know your enemy." I say, "Know your client."

Online, in direct mail, in any kind of advertising, this is obvious. Before you create any advert, you first consider who you're advertising to. Because if you're advertising to everyone, you reach no-one.

Why?

We're not all interested in the same things. We don't all pay attention to the same things. We all weigh the same information differently.

We each have a small bundle of nerve endings in our brains, known as the Reticular Activating System (RAS).

The RAS is often described as the brain's bouncer. It's the part that filters out excess sensory stimulation, so you don't become overwhelmed.

It's also the brain's secretary, deciding which bits of information get passed to the conscious mind.

Certain things have a VIP pass and will always

waltz right by your RAS gatekeeper like an A-lister at an after party.

If it's link to self-preservation or procreation, it will get your attention. That's why sex sells.

For everything else, getting through is a bit tougher. But what generally gets through are things we are currently interested in, or things that challenge or reinforce a deeply held belief.

It's like when you buy a new car, you suddenly see how many others of that make and model are on the road.

When you're in a crowded room with a lot of background noise, the RAS filters it out so you don't become overwhelmed with sensory input.

Yet if someone says your name, you hear it distinctly from all those other sounds. If someone you have a crush on speaks, you hear their voice over all the others.

And if someone you have a crush on says your name, you'll have a hard time focusing on anyone else standing right in front of you, right?

At its simplest, it helps you find the items you like on a restaurant menu and filter out those you don't quickly.

But how does that help you get more sales?

Well, sex may sell, but it isn't always appropriate. Overuse of shock tactics will quickly turn your clients off, not on.

Similarly, you can't be all doom and gloom all the time, or always play on fearful emotions.

You need to know what will get through your clients' RAS, and what will get bounced and filtered out.

What you want to do is extract as much information from your clients as possible. Particularly, what their hobbies and interests are. What are their "hot buttons"?

Everybody has them. Those subjects that make them light up, that once they start talking about, it's hard to shut them up.

Once you know what those subjects are, make a note. Create lists of people who like the same things, and share content with them about their hot topics, even if they're nothing to do with your business.

In short, find out what they want, then give it to them.

Serve a Niche, Solve a Problem

If you try to appeal to everyone, and avoid offending anyone, you'll end up bland, boring and broke! You'll be undistinguishable from everyone else out there.

The real power of choosing a niche is in identifying an audience you can talk to in a way that makes them love you.

Fair warning: when you do that, you will inevitably make other people hate you. That's okay.

Don't worry about trying to appeal to everyone. Just identify your audience.

Who already listens to you? Who likes what you have to say?

If you talk to those people effectively enough, you will have all the followers you ever need.

And if you do it really well, they will talk to and "convert" enough other people on your behalf that you will attract people outside your audience.

Let's say for example, you want to sell around search engine optimisation (SEO) services.

You can't talk to everyone who runs a website, the audience and diversity of needs is too great.

So, you narrow down your audience to a niche.

Combine your SEO knowledge with another interest or industry.

Write about SEO for Doctors, SEO for music tutors, or SEO for haulage companies.

You can then create content that uses their language, and specifically target that group in your marketing.

But identifying your audience is only half the answer. You also need to work out what problem you're solving for them.

The problems a haulage company has with SEO might be different from those a music instructor or doctor has.

Yes, they all want to increase their website's visibility in search engine results pages.

So does everyone. That's too generic.

Think about the problems in SEO that are specific to doctors, such as providing content using non-medical terms patients might use and including correct disclaimers to avoid medical malpractice suits.

What problems might music tutors have?

If they're teaching kids, they need to appeal to two audiences; the kids who want to learn an instrument, and the parents who will be paying for the lessons.

A haulage company has the challenge of selling B2B but needing content that appeals to individuals.

These are by no means the only issues. But identifying the main ones and picking one problem you can help solve for your audience will help you stand out.

You'll become the Trucker's SEO Guy. Or the SEO Doctor.

Focus on providing what those who are following you want.

If you try to cover too much or have products and services that aren't closely related to each other, many people will think your product or service is diluted, and you're not an expert.

Don't do that. Don't mainstream your message, focus on the niche.

If you focus on serving a small crowd to the best of your ability, and that crowd loves your product or service, they will rave about you so much, your audience grows, and what once was a niche can become mainstream.

Apple was a niche. The apple and iMac were a niche product. The iPod was a niche.

What made those products go mainstream wasn't the company trying to appeal to a wider audience.

It was a small but dedicated group of people who were so invested in their attachment to the Apple brand, they talked about their gadgets incessantly.

They showed them off. They bragged about them, and slowly converted their friends, who converted their friends, and so on.

Go for your niche market. Focus on finding your crowd that gets you and talking to them.

Who's on Your List?

Sales and marketing experts will tell you, "The money is in the list."

What does that mean?

It means having a list of people who want to hear from you is always more profitable than trying to market to people who have never heard of you.

Think about it this way, if you have a new product, who are more likely to buy from you:

- Complete strangers, who have never heard of you
- Existing customers, and people who know, like, and trust you

Obviously, it's existing customers, and people who know, like, and trust you. They're your crowd.

But to sell to that crowd, you need to know who they are and how to reach them. That's why it's important to start building your master list from the outset.

Wherever you are, and whatever you do, always carry business cards, and talk about your business.

Get the conversation started by asking people what they do and be sincere and genuinely interested.

Don't be focused on how soon you can turn the conversation to you. Listen to them and learn from them.

Then when they get around to asking you what you do, have your elevator speech practiced and be able to tell them in a couple of sentences what you do, and what your angle is.

If they have any interest, give them a card, invite them for a free lesson/sample/session, and give them options, but close on them. Make an appointment. Bring them in.

When they say yes, because you're giving them something for free, get their name, phone, and email, and let them know there's something you want to send them, and then make it good.

One great way to do this is with the QR code on the back of the card. You can give it to them, explain the deal, and get them to scan the code right then, and enter their email address.

When you collect emails for your list, remember you're also doing it for networking, not just broadcasting.

If you're working online, use a list management service like Mailchimp, aWebber, or GetResponse to collect email addresses and send out scheduled and broadcast emails.

Use a double opt-in system, so you can't be accused of spamming people, and only send high-value information to people on your list.

But stay in regular contact with them, so they don't forget who you are and why they signed up to receive email from you.

If they glaze over, let them be. They're not your audience. They don't want your pen.

You don't need a massive list to generate sales. Maintaining a list has time and cost implications, so don't try to collect the whole world's contact details.

A small, tightly focused list populated with your tribe, eager to hear from you, and ready to buy, will outperform a larger list with no points of commonality.

If you're selling SEO services to doctors, you want a list of medical professionals. If you're selling to music tutors, you want musicians.

Build Your Own Sales Funnel

Just as you need to build your own list, and focus on your own audience, you need your own sales funnel and content, even if you're working for someone else.

You could be selling 10, 20, 30 times more than you do now with an effective sales funnel.

Unfortunately, most corporate sales funnels are generic, and unfocused. You also can't take them with you and adapt them to a new product if you switch companies.

Think of your employer as a supplier. If they go under, they don't have to take you with them. You can take your content and your list and find a new supplier to solve your audience's problem.

A funnel doesn't have to be massively complex, though. Let me show you one of my early funnels.

I had two books. *Success! Improvise, Adapt, Overcome* and *The Closers Part 3* with Ben Gay III. These books were both sold online at major retailers. They were available in book stores, and we sold directly from our websites.

Initially I tried to sell the books directly with paid marketing, but it didn't go too well.

So, I started giving away one of the books as a lead magnet in a sales funnel.

I made a landing page at SuccessIAO.com, and drove traffic to that page from Facebook, Twitter, YouTube, and other sources.

The page allowed users to download a free version of the eBook in exchange for their email address.

Once they entered their email address, they would be sent to a thank you page with the download link, and a link to the option to get a paperback copy from their favourite retailer.

After that, they would receive a series of emails every three days, with related valuable free content. I would give them success tips, quotes and memes, and I would direct them to YouTube videos of mine relating to the book, and back to social media accounts where they could get more things for free by following me.

This builds rapport, gives the reader a lot of value, and here and there the option to buy a hard copy of the book.

But when they have gone through the sequence, they also receive an email that asks them if they are interested in sales and gives them a link to a video on how to get more sales.

If they watch the video, they're moved to a list for readers who are interested in sales. If not, they stay on the list they're on, and continue to get free success emails.

They're basically staying on the list to receive success clippings, until I have something else to offer them.

The funnel is a way to get people onto your lists and keep in contact with them until you find something of interest to offer them.

You might offer a free lead magnet, and then a low-priced first product. But free lead magnets attract freebie hunters who often download the freebie and unsubscribe from the list without ever reading the freebie.

Offering a low-cost introductory product, such as a book or report, is often a better idea. It positions you in a new subscriber's mind as a seller, not just a giver.

Provided you deliver value and a positive customer experience, people who buy from you once are more likely to buy in the future than those who only stay on your list for free stuff.

Don't wait too long to offer your free list subscribers the opportunity to make the switch to paying customers. Otherwise, you condition them to think of you as a source of free information. They will assume you make your money from advertising, not sales.

Trying to escape the "free info" slot in your subscribers' minds can be a bit like trying to get out of the "friend zone" with a crush you waited too long to make a move on, because you were too shy or insecure.

You think you're laying the groundwork for a possible relationship, and they've assumed you just want to be friends.

Nightmare.

Don't build your list like a "Freebie friend." Be a "Sexy seller." You may build your list and your network slower, but it will consist of higher quality connections who are prepared to invest in themselves and buy from you.

From that low-cost initial product, you can offer a product ladder, from courses and more in-depth reports, to classes, workshops, coaching and consulting, to speaking and training. Or whatever sales ladder makes sense for you.

Although I write books, I never wanted to be just an author. The books are one part of my strategy, but they feed into other things.

I have had invitations to speak, training gigs, and consulting positions all come from my books. I have been invited to collaborate on videos with other YouTube influencers, to guest on podcasts, and to collaborate on other books.

Many of these invitations would never have come if I hadn't written the books. But they also wouldn't have come if I hadn't used the books to build my list and grow my connections. If I had simply published the books and sat back, they wouldn't have worked for me the way they have.

At its simplest, your funnel should consist of a Landing Page, which makes an Offer, a Subscription form, and a List, hosted with a mail service. Then you drive traffic to the landing page.

There's a science to building an effective landing page.

Go to SuccessIAO.com or TheClosers3.com and

see my sales funnels in action. They're simple, and they work.

On the pages, you will see sales copy and a video. The videos are made to sell, and they work, because they follow the sales process.

If you take these tips and create a sales funnel and landing page like mine for your own products, you will start to build a list of interested followers who are ready to buy from you when you have something to offer them.

And if you're worried about building a landing page, don't be. You don't need technical knowledge.

You can use a service such as Get Response, Landing Pages, or Click Funnels to quickly build hosted pages and connect them to your mail service provider.

How to Sell on the Phone

With everybody using social media these days, is it even worth learning to close on the phone and cold calling?

Most people use social media because it's efficient, it's fun, and it's easy. No one likes tedious and hard, right? Especially when it means you have to call someone you don't know. It's intimidating.

No one likes sales calls, right? You're having fun, or concentrating on a project, and the phone rings. Its incessant noise won't quit until you do something about it. Your concentration is shattered.

When you do answer it, as soon as you hear an unfamiliar voice, you ask yourself, "What do you want, and what's it going to cost me?"

Then some stranger wants to know everything from your star sign to your inside leg measurements, so you can prove who you are before they empty your bank account, right?

But it works.

It works because it's disruptive.

Because it reaches real people in real time, without long-distance travel. Because it's quick.

Because most people are backing away from cold calling, you can use it and take market share.

Here's the problem with social media. Yes, you can make a post with your pitch and share it.

But if someone has an objection, they're not always going to ask a question.

They're not even going to answer, "I have to think about it."

They're just going to scroll past.

Which means you'll never even know they saw it.

And that's assuming the site served your post to them in the first place, and it didn't get drowned out by all the other posts within seconds.

On social media, you don't hear objections. You hear crickets. It's silent rejection.

At least if you get someone on the phone and hear those objections, you have an opportunity to overcome them, and make a sale.

But it only works if you know how to do it right.

First, if you're selling business to business, you're going to make calls during office hours.

But also call outside those hours. Call before nine in the morning, and after five in the evening.

Think about it. Who works nine to five?

Employees. Gatekeepers. Secretaries. Boss blockers.

People who don't make buying decisions.

Who stays late, and arrives early? Often, it's the CEO, the owner, the boss.

Who do you want to reach? When's the best time to reach them?

Now, when you're talking on the phone, smile. Even though the other person can't see you smile, they can hear it in your voice. It changes your tone and your energy.

Stand up to make calls. When you're standing up, you're more confident and powerful. You move around, you're more expressive, you think faster.

Standing opens up your chest and clears your airways, so you project your voice better. It also makes you feel in control because you can move around.

If you're sitting down, you're constrained. You feel weaker, your chest is closed, and your voice won't project as well. Stand up and feel your energy flowing.

Before you make any calls, think about those two questions you ask when you hear an unfamiliar voice.

What do you want?

What's it going to cost me?

Be sure you can frame your answers to those questions in a positive light. Turn them around.

What does your client want?

How can you deliver it?

Remember those problems we talked about? The ones your audience has that you can solve? You want to open with those.

So, let's say you're selling SEO marketing to driving instructors. Your potential client doesn't want to talk to you because he's on his way to pick up a client, and if he's late, it could cost him money.

If you pitch him, "Hi, my name's Paul, and I'm calling from SellAPen SEO Services. I'd like to discuss your local marketing with you, and explain how we can..."

It doesn't matter what you can... you already lost him. Tell him,

"Hi, Jim. I've been looking at your local marketing spend and results, and I think you're spending far more than you need to for too little return."

Now you have his attention. You're alerting him to a potential problem. It's personal to him, and you're immediately in the role of advisor, not salesperson.

Tell him, "Look I know your time is valuable, I'd like to run through your options with you so we can fix this."

Then do an alternative close, "Do you want to talk about this right now or tomorrow at 4?"

Your chances of setting the appointment are much higher than if you say something like, "I'd like to come and see you to explain our services what do you think?"

When setting appointments on the phone, give two options. So, ask "Would six pm Monday work for you, or would you prefer 7 pm Tuesday?"

If he says neither are possible, instead of offering an alternative day, ask if it's a time issue, or a scheduling one.

If you're trying to schedule an hour-long appointment, and your customer only has half an hour to spare, he's not going to meet with you. Tell him you'll keep it short, if you can, and then stick to the time allocated.

If he has an hour to meet you, but no time to travel, arrange to go to him.

If it's a simple scheduling issue, and he's only available on Monday, but already has a six o'clock appointment, tell him you'll rearrange something and meet him for lunch, or stretch your evening hours and meet him at nine.

But don't keep chasing alternative times, because that makes you sound desperate, and as though you have no other appointments.

If you're struggling to get a time commitment, take the initiative away. Say, "Look let's make this work. When do you want to meet? Or do you want to let this opportunity go? Do you want to keep losing money?"

Above all, speak with the assumption that the meeting will be to his benefit. You're there to fix his problem, and if he doesn't fix it, it's going to keep getting worse.

How to Meet and Greet

The meet and greet is how you approach somebody. It's how you walk up to them, how you introduce yourself. How you win them over right from the beginning.

You only have one chance to make a first impression, right?

Back in my timeshare days, we used to have a sales deck. Couples would wait for us in reception. They were called in to receive a free gift, which was a free holiday.

Their only requirement to get the holiday was to attend a 90-minute presentation on timeshare.

It was our job, in those 90 minutes, to sell it to them.

You can, of course, apply this in any industry.

First, if the client has come to see you, you approach them walk with confidence.

"Hi, Paul." Smile, and hold out your hand.

If you have gone to see them, smile and introduce yourself, but don't hold your hand out unless they do. You're already in their space, and going for the handshake can be seen as pushy. This is particularly true if you're selling B2C or door to door.

If it's a mixed-sex couple, make sure you greet the one who is the same sex as you first. This reduces any tension or jealousy that can otherwise ripple under the surface.

Shake hands with a firm grip, again approaching the same-sex member first. When you greet the opposite sex member, give marginally less time to them, again to reduce any chance of jealousy.

When you walk clients into the presentation room or your office, direct them where to sit. In some cases, this is obvious; you're not going to have a client sit behind your desk while you sit in a guest chair, right?

But where seating is more open plan, taking charge and seating clients is even more important.

For one thing, you want to be able to look at and give them both (or all if there are more than two) reasonably equal attention, without giving yourself a stiff neck.

When you direct them where to sit, do it with your whole hand, palm facing up, not with your index finger pointing.

There's a difference in how this is perceived. Instead of ordering them around, you're being the gracious host, and inviting them to take a seat, while maintaining control.

Although it's subtle, it also affects your voice.

How to Meet and Greet

Just test this. The next time you get the chance, point to a chair with your index finger and say, "Sit there."

Then try it with your palm up, and be aware of how different you sound. Also notice how the gesture is received.

When you seat them, seat the same-sex person beside you, and the opposite sex one opposite you, if you're at a square table.

Sit next to the same sex customer. Again, this avoids any inadvertent inappropriate touching and eliminates jealousy from the other partner.

Sit so that you're not blocking their view when you're writing. So, if you're right-handed, sit to their left. If you're left-handed, sit to their right. This keeps your body posture open to them.

If you're not going to be writing, sit to their right. Subconsciously, we give more attention to things and people on our right.

Don't seat clients opposite each other, because then you have to split your attention between them.

It also makes it easier for them to communicate behind your back. While you're looking at one partner, they're looking at each other, and sharing hand signals.

You might be talking to the wife, and she's saying, "oh, that sounds lovely," but all the while behind your back, the husband is making throat slitting gestures.

Once you've got them seated, you move into your warm up. You want to get them relaxed. You don't want to start a sales presentation with clients sitting arms crossed. It's a sign they're closed to you and feeling defensive.

There are lots of ways to get someone to open their arms and move them towards a more open body language.

One quick way is to give them a brochure or something to look at. They have to uncross their arms to take it from you.

But then you have to take it back from them to regain their attention. Otherwise they might just flip through the brochure and not listen to what you have to say.

While you can do a take-away to achieve that, if they're feeling defensive, it could backfire.

Another way to open someone's posture and reduce friction is to compliment them on something, and if appropriate ask them to take a look.

You might say, "Hey, is that the latest iPhone? Can I see it?"

He has to unfold his arms to show you, and to take it back from you. Before he has chance to close back up again, you can lead him into something else that keeps him open. You might touch his hand or forearm lightly.

What do you talk about in your warmup?

In timeshare sales, I would talk about holidays, jobs, and kids.

Holidays, because that's what we were selling, and everyone loves holidays, right? Very few people don't like them, so they're a safe, positive, upbeat conversation topic that's on point.

Talk about their jobs. And no matter what they do, be interested. Don't act interested. Be interested. It doesn't matter what they do, there's always something you can learn or ask about.

Say you meet a plumber. Take the opportunity to learn a few things about plumbing. If there's nothing you always wanted to know about plumbing but had no one to ask, ask about the pay, the hours, the working environment. If none of that works, ask about the people they meet, and the stories they have to share.

Every job has them.

Not only will you learn new things, you'll be entertained with funny stories, and have plenty to talk about with your friends – not to mention the next plumber you meet.

Ask questions. Smile. If you make a joke, even if it's one you make all the time and you don't think it's that funny anymore say it with a smile, and even laugh a little.

Just because you hear it every day, doesn't mean they do.

Even if your laugh is a little fake, it signals humour to the other person, and gives them permission to laugh.

Even if they don't find it funny, so long as you're not offensive, the chances are they will smile to be polite.

And what happens when they smile? The same

thing that happens when you smile at yourself in the mirror, even though you don't want to.

Just as smiling makes you happier, getting your clients smiling makes them start to feel good and relax. Even if it's a fake smile.

If you keep your presentations light-hearted, smile, crack a joke or two, and get them laughing, people will be more willing to buy from you.

Remember to include both, or all, customers in the presentation. Don't sell to the person you think is the decision maker and ignore everyone else – you might be surprised at the end to learn the one who controls the purse strings isn't the one you thought.

Compliment people. Do it sincerely, and evenly. Don't heap praise on one person and throw the other a token comment. You can always find something to compliment someone on, even if it's their hair, shoes, tie, etc.

There's no set script for this. But there are a few basic rules you can follow.

Talk to people about their kids if they have them, hobbies and interests if not. Get people to tell you about their hopes and dreams.

Get them talking.

Once you get them talking, listen.

The Trump Handshake

Love him or hate him, it's hard to miss Donald Trump's handshake. It's distinctive.

You only have one chance to make a first impression, and it can make or break a business deal. Your handshake is one of the most important, and often overlooked, factors.

The handshake releases oxytocin. Oxytocin regulates social interaction, and sexual behaviour.

Hey, how you doin'?

There are three main types of positions – when you're shaking hands: vertical, under-palm, and overpalm.

All three positions trigger subliminal reactions.

When you shake hands vertically, it's equal, and people feel comfortable with you. When you shake with your palm facing down (overpalm) it's dominant.

People will think you are trying to control them or trying to get something from them. This usually raises a red flag.

Conversely, if you shake someone's hand with your palm facing up, it's submissive, and people think they can get one over on you. They think you are weak.

What you want to do is shake someone's hand with a vertical palm, equally.

What I tend to do, because it's the way I was taught many years ago before I understood the psychology, is to have a slight overpalm handshake, but not so much that people notice.

But if someone tries to overpalm you, there are counter handshakes. There are many, but here are my favourites.

- When someone tries to overpalm you, take a step forward, shifting your weight onto your left leg. It naturally twists your body, but also moves you into the overpalmer's personal space. This naturally puts you in the position of power.
- If the overpalming is almost horizontal, put your other hand on top of his and shake double-handed. You see this a lot with politicians, because it puts the double-handed shaker in the position of power while looking friendly and warm.

Which bring us to Donald Trump's distinctive double handshake.

When someone tries to overpalm Trump, he pulls them towards him, into his space, and then taps them lightly in a double-hand shake, and then tugs them again.

This has the natural result of throwing the other person off balance and making them look awkward while making Trump look dominant.

But what's the best way to shake somebody's hand – if you don't want it to turn into a power struggle?

Put your hand out vertically, smile, and introduce yourself.

But I'm a big guy, and I can come across intimidating. So, when I shake someone's hand who is smaller than me, especially women, I usually bow a little.

Bowing actually shows confidence, power, and friendliness.

Shake three times and release. The amount of pressure you apply should be the same as your partner.

Because you don't want to be too close or too standoffish, it's best to let the other person set the distance between you when shaking.

A lot of people recommend the double hand shake, but if the other person doesn't know you, this can seem fake and intrusive.

Many sales trainers also suggest you put your hand out first. Do NOT do this. Let me explain why.

If you're selling door to door, and you go to someone's door and you reach out first, it's very intrusive. It annoys people and raises all kinds of red flags.

If you're having pictures taken, or being filmed, you want to be standing on the left side.

Remember, people naturally give more attention to people and things on the right, so you want to be on the right of the picture. But photos are reversed, so you need to stand on the left.

You will naturally look more dominant and more powerful. This is another thing many politicians try to do. JFK. Was a master at it.

JFK understood how to use body language, and that gave him a hug advantage, and ultimately the presidency.

The election presidential debates between Nixon and JFK was the first one ever televised. Here's a funny thing; people surveyed who listened to the debates on the radio thought that Nixon won the debate and would be the next president, independent of who they supported.

People who saw the debates on TV believed that JFK won the debate and would be the next president, again irrespective of their own support.

I can't guarantee understanding handshakes and body language will earn you a presidency, but it will improve your bottom line.

How to Make People Like You

We've already talked about how people buy from people they know, like, and trust. They can't buy from you if they don't know about you.

Given a choice, they will buy from the person they like most, but will still do business with someone they don't like much if they have trust.

But we also tend to trust people we like, due to the halo effect cognitive bias, in which we assume that someone who has one good trait or feature also possesses other, not necessarily related, traits and features.

So, once you have introduced yourself to people, and they know you, you can help them to like and trust you.

Are you ready for the secret to how?

Are you sure?

This is powerful stuff. It can literally skyrocket your income and exponentially increase your sales.

Don't be fooled by how deceptively simple it sounds.

Do these few things, and people will like and trust you.

- Be sincere
- Be transparent
- Be honest
- Be confident

Apart from the basics of being polite, punctual, reliable, honest, and looking presentable, it's easy to think people either like you or they don't.

But you can help people to like you without being fake or resorting to dishonesty.

One simple way is to mirror their body language. Smile when they smile, nod when they nod, agree with them.

Be open.

Don't fold your arms and scowl.

Don't scratch your head and keep your hands away from your face. We interpret scratching the nose as indecision, covering the mouth as dishonesty, and most other hand-to-face gestures as a sign of weakness or deceit in one way or another.

On camera, have something in the background that makes people smile, like a picture of a kitten, or a figurine from a popular TV show. Let your personality shine through in your surroundings.

People who like the same things as you will feel affinity for you even before you speak.

Start with a compliment

Always open a conversation on a positive note. Whether it's with a compliment or a general observation, never start a conversation with a negative.

If it's great weather, start with that. If it's terrible, ignore it. If you got stuck in traffic and you're late, open with a positive before you explain. Find something to comment on, whether it's the artwork on the wall, the landscaping, someone's clothing, or something interesting you passed on the way.

Give compliments. You don't have to be fake and flatter. Give genuine compliments. There's always something you can find to like about someone, even if it's only their shoes or their jacket.

Be positive

Wherever you can, ignore the negative. Where you can't ignore it, frame it in a positive light.

And where you can't ignore it or reframe it, address it briefly and move on to something more positive.

You've probably heard "Never talk ill about competitors," but no one ever explains why – other than its unprofessional.

Here's why. Your brain doesn't function the way you think it does.

If you say to someone, "This guy is so

unprofessional, he's cheap, and he's always late," their brain will automatically associate the words, "unprofessional, cheap, and late" with you.

Not the other person you're talking about.

You.

The negatives you try to associate to someone else end up attached to you. You jeopardise your reputation, and it looks tacky.

If your client bashes your competition, don't be tempted to join in.

Just smile, and say, "I can't comment on that," or keep your comments about yourself.

Take a genuine interest

You need to ask questions to learn about your customer's needs. You also need to make small talk to break the ice and build rapport.

But you can't do this by rote, and not listen to the answers, and expect people to like you.

Give people your full attention when you're talking to them.

Clarify your understanding of what they're telling you by paraphrasing what they just told you.

This isn't just an important part of the job if you want to make sales.

It a vital part of communication in life.

Misunderstandings occur because people mishear, misinterpret or plain fail to pay enough attention.

Nobody likes being ignored. Nobody likes being served by a cashier who is too busy talking on the phone to count out your change correctly. Or having to repeat themselves because the other person didn't listen the first time.

If you want people to like you, you have to genuinely like people.

Something to live up to

When you give someone a label, they tend to live up, or down, to that.

So, if you tell someone they are smart, they feel smart. If you tell someone they are funny, they will feel funny.

The strange thing is, if you tell someone they're funny, they also tend to try to crack jokes throughout the conversation, trying to live up to the label you gave them.

Use this to your benefit. Tell people they are decisive.

In timeshare, I would handle this up front I would say something like, "You look like and intelligent couple. You seem like you can take decisions for your own family, yes?"

When they agree, because I fed them the "Yes," I would use that to get the commitment to making a decision that day, and locking out the, "I want to think about it," objection.

You can also use someone's profession to associate decisiveness to them.

When you ask someone what they do, if the job they tell you is one with responsibility, you can say, "That's a lot of responsibility. So, you have to make some tough decisions, right? At least I know I'm going to get a decision from you today, and you're not going to give me excuses, right?"

Always end on a high note

Have you ever eaten out, and had the wait staff bring you a tray with a complimentary mint or chocolate after your meal but before the bill?

They're not just being nice.

Studies have shown that those complimentary mints increase tips for the wait staff.

If they leave you one, start to walk away, return, and leave you two, those same studies have shown it makes the customer feel special, and increases the tip even more.

At the end of your presentation, give your clients a wrapped chocolate. This not only makes them feel special, it increases your chances of closing the deal.

It also gives you a barometer to tell how they're feeling.

If they unwrap the chocolate and eat it, they're feeling good, and feeling safe. And eating the chocolate will increase those feelings, so you're more likely to get the sale.

In prehistoric times, people would only eat when they were in a safe environment, because it distracted them from the possibility of attack by predators. Our reptile brains still associate eating with safety.

So, if we're feeling stressed, we won't eat. And if we do eat, that increases our sense of safety.

Plus, of course, chocolate produces feel-good endorphins.

So now they're feeling good, they're feeling safe, and they like you more.

Your chances of closing the deal went up.

How to sell anyone anything

We are always selling something.

Think about it.

Interviews, products, advertising, ideas. You're always selling something, right?

When you interview for a job, you're selling your experience and talent.

When you call in sick, you're selling the boss your excuse.

When you ask for a raise, you're selling them on remembering all your good points and overlooking your faults.

Even in your personal life, you're always selling something.

When you meet someone new, you're selling them on you, as a colleague, friend, or potential partner.

When you propose, you're selling your partner on gambling on life with you being a good investment of time, energy, and emotion.

If you're a parent, you're constantly selling your kids on eating the right food, getting dressed, doing homework.

And they're constantly selling you on what constitutes the right food, the latest toy craze, and staying up late.

Selling, selling, selling.

I'm going to give you a formula that will be a foundation, so you can always get that sale.

And the last tip I give you will literally make you buy your own product. Every time.

Promise

The first phase of any sale is the promise, and it's designed to hook your prospect. You have five to ten seconds to hook your prospect, whether it's on the phone or face to face. Much less if you're on line.

That's how long you have to hook someone and make them want to hear you out.

This applies to cold calling, commercials, movies – in fact those first few seconds are one of the most important things in a movie trailer.

It's the promise of what you're going to see, what you're going to get. Why should you stick around? What's in it for you?

This will set the tone and expectation for the rest of your commercial, pitch, presentation, movie, or whatever.

The hook in this book is to show you how to use simple psychology to get your own way and close the deal.

Sell the sizzle

You've probably heard the saying, "Don't sell the steak, sell the sizzle."

Chances are, you probably also understand that to mean, "Don't sell the features, sell the benefits."

But what does that mean in real terms? Do you even know the difference between features and benefits?

For those of you who don't, features are the physical attributes of a product, or the terms of a service. Benefits are the advantages of those features.

But I'm going to make it easy for you.

Sell the sizzle, at base, means sell the emotions, the sensory experience, and the memories.

What are they going to feel? Smell? Taste? See? Hear?

Try this, with apologies to vegetarians. You may need to imagine a fat, juicy mushroom steak instead.

If I say to you, "I fancy a steak," what do you imagine?

Maybe a piece of meat on a plate. Possibly the fries and salad that go with it.

But if I say to you, "I fancy a steak. Medium rare, swimming in gravy, with a drizzle of blue cheese sauce, a pile of steaming fries, and a salad of peppery spinach and rocket, sweet cherry tomatoes, and sliced Spanish onions," you're starting to get a more detailed picture.

But is that really selling the sizzle? Or just painting a more detailed picture of a steak?

How about if I say, "I'm hungry. I fancy a gut-busting steak. Cooked to perfection, melt-in-the-mouth texture, with a perfect sauce and sides."

Notice how here, I'm letting you fill in the details, and focusing on the experience, after first stating the problem.

Can you imagine the smell? Can you imagine the taste?

See how strong that is in your mind right now?

Think about what you're selling – the steak.

Break that down to the features – a 10 oz rump steak, for example is a prime cut.

List the benefits. Rump steak is ideal for slow cooking, cheaper, and tastier than sirloin, for example.

Take that one step further. What are the benefits of the benefits?

- If it's cheaper, you save money,
- tastier means more satisfying,
- and slow-cooking means you can spend less time standing over it and get on with other things.

So it's better value, a better experience, and more convenient.

Keep in mind, when people go to a hardware store, to buy a drill, what do they buy? They don't buy the drill. They buy the hole they want to make in the wall.

On a deeper level, what they're really buying is the feeling that the hole will give them when they hang a picture on it of their family.

Get testimonials

You need social proof. The cognitive bias the Bandwagon Effect leads us to believe things because other people believe them.

We will even doubt our own judgement if enough other people voice an alternative opinion.

And don't tell them the proof, show them.

You can do this by literally showing them the proof, or by painting the picture in their mind.

For example, you can build credibility by showing what your customers say about you on review sites.

Or you can get an endorsement from a trusted third party.

When I wrote my first book, *Success!* I had been in business for twenty years. I had been the youngest sales reps, sales manager and then sales trainer in one of the largest timeshare and holiday sales companies in Europe.

I had also owned and run my own nightclub and co-owned a recruitment agency in Bulgaria focusing on construction.

Despite this, I was mostly known as an entertainer and video production manager in Greece, and relatively unknown outside the country.

Determined to reach a wider audience, I made the risky decision to write and publish in English.

That meant a lot of my potential audience wouldn't have heard of me, and a lot of my existing audience wouldn't be able to read my books.

So, I approached a senior sales trainer and author, Ben Gay III, who had become a mentor to me some time before, to write the foreword for me, as social proof.

That went so well, it led to a collaboration with the living legend and author of the famous blue books of sales on *The Closers - Part III.*

Now in sales circles, I can establish my credibility instantly just by sharing my back catalogue.

Ben Gay III doesn't endorse just anyone.

Let alone write a follow-up to books that had sold millions of copies (*The Closers - Part 1* had sold over 20 million when they stopped counting several years ago) with them.

To those in the know, having worked with Ben Gay III is a door-opener.

- Who are the influencers in your industry?
- Who are your most supportive clients?
- Who will give you recommendations and endorsement?
- Who will vouch for you?

Reach out to these people. If you use LinkedIn.com, they have a built-in function to ask for recommendations. Use that to collect endorsements that you can take with you throughout your career. Get their support in writing and share it.

But don't just think in terms of testimonials. Think collaborations. Interview the influencers in your industry and share the videos on your YouTube channel.

Have you picture taken with thought leaders. Put those pictures on the wall where clients who will recognise those people can see them.

The pitch

I'm going to give you one word to remember when you give a sales presentation so that you can close it every time.

KISS.

Keep It Stupid Simple. (I prefer that to Keep It Simple, Stupid, because I don't believe you're stupid.)

Say you're selling a car, and your customer wants to know about the engine.

You don't need to open the bonnet and start describing the engine in detail like a mechanic.

Unless he's a petrol head, he doesn't care (and if he he's he'll be the one telling you.)

Your customer wants to know how many girls he's going to pull with this car. He wants to know if it's going to be safe to drive for his family, or how fast he can get to work.

The more time you spend telling him things he doesn't want to know, the more likely he is to lose interest. And the more technical you get, the more questions he will have.

Then, because you've overloaded him with information and confused him, he's going to say he wants to think about it.

Think about it.

If he wants to think about it, it's because you confused him.

It's not your job to confuse him, it's your job to clarify things. Keep that in mind.

What are you selling?

Without reading ahead, take a few minutes to explain what you sell. Stand up, shake your shoulders, get some energy in you, and say out loud what you're selling.

Did you do it?

No?

STOP!

How to Sell a Pen Really

I don't care if you don't do any of the other exercises in the book, do this one before you continue.

Seriously. Just do it.

Now did you do it?

Okay.

Now write it down:

"I am selling_____

_____

_____

_____

_____

_____

_____

_____

_____

_____

_____

_____

_____."

If you said you're selling a product or service, think again. That's just what you have to offer.

If you described the features of the product or service, go back and do it again. That's just a description.

If you listed the benefits of the product or service, well done, but you're not quite right.

You don't sell cartoon network, you're selling the smile parents see their kids have when watching it.

You don't sell movies subscription, you sell the feeling you get watching a movie with your wife after a long day at work when kids are asleep.

You don't sell the game, you sell the laughter and shouting with your friends (imagine commercials)

Even if you followed the line to the end and listed the benefits of the benefits, the experience your customers will enjoy, the problem you solve, or the transformation you will help them achieve, that's still not what you're selling.

So, what are you really selling?

If you answered anything other than "yourself," you're making a mistake.

People buy you.

Yes, you.

People buy because they like you.

Do you know how many times my sales reps on the phone hear, "I'm buying it because of you," or

"I'm buying it because I like you."

So, what are you selling, exactly?

You are selling your confidence, your expertise. You're selling you.

To do that, you need to believe in yourself, and you need to know that you can sell anything.

You can, of course, because you're selling yourself. So, the underlying product never changes.

Do you buy yourself?

If not, go back to the seven daily habits, and keep working on your mindset until you do.

Anchoring

Another method to help you encourage people to feel good about you, and like you, is anchoring.

To explain this, I'm going to talk in terms of flirting with someone you like.

It works in sales, too, but in sales where you're building a relationship with a client whose account you manage, or where you're making a long-term sale for a big-ticket item, or as a preferred supplier or contractor.

This isn't something that will work on single presentation sales, such as door-to-door or retail.

On your first date, you want to take your partner to a bar. You don't want to go for a meal – where there's a barrier between you, or to the movies – where your attention isn't on each other.

You want to go somewhere where you can have fun, communicate, and touch.

That's because touching releases oxytocin in their brain. Oxytocin is a neurotransmitter that promotes positive feelings.

Your aim is to get your partner to relax, and to feel good. So, whenever you say something funny, or whenever they laugh, lightly touch their arm, below the elbow. It's non-threatening.

You don't want to be pawing at someone you just met or lurching across the room to reach them, so you only do this when it's natural and easy to do.

And don't go slapping people on the shoulder or punching them on the arm. That's just another way to end up with a few loose teeth and no sales or second dates.

If you touch someone and they pull away or frown, don't keep trying to use touch to anchor positive feelings; it won't work. Unwanted touch may release stress hormones instead and be counterproductive.

But as time goes on, every time they laugh or smile, and it's natural, you touch them. What happens is their brain starts to associate your touch with the laughter. Your touch becomes associated with feeling good.

You're anchoring the association with your touch to feeling safe and feeling good.

It's the same with clients. The more you touch them in a non-threatening, natural way when you or they say something funny, and you're both smiling or laughing, the more they will warm to you.

In time, people begin to associate your touch with feeling good, and that's when you start to have some influence over them.

Because they associate your touch with feeling good, they will start to feel good when you touch them. They will feel safe.

Now, you can touch them on the elbow at the end of the pitch, and say, "Its a good deal, Jim."

That might be all the push they need when done right

Don't abuse that trust. There are things you can use to influence people that can also be used to manipulate them. You might get away with it for a while if you have bad intent, but it won't work for long.

And as a side note, if you're in any kind of relationship with someone who treats you badly, but you notice you feel good when they touch you, be aware they may have conditioned you, and you need to step away from that relationship.

How to persuade anyone

The best and most effective way to convince anyone of anything is to let them do the convincing for you. What do I mean by that?

I mean, if you try to persuade someone of something, they will resist your efforts, and distrust you. They will feel as though you are trying to manipulate them.

If, instead, you simply present them with information in certain ways designed to appeal to well-known thought patterns, the outcomes are predictable.

But the customer feels as though they have arrived at their own conclusions and decisions.

Because they have, with a little help from psychology, heuristics, and cognitive biases.

Heuristics are strategies that use known information to fill in gaps in novel situations, to help us make decisions better and faster.

But they're also a form of intellectual shorthand. They are thought patterns which have developed over the course of human evolution to reduce the number of conscious decisions we have to make in the face of uncertainty, too much or not enough information, and time constraints.

Although they are illogical and flawed, they have developed, and we cling to them because most of the time they work to our benefit. Without them, we would be paralyzed by indecision.

In other words, they are gut feelings, hunches, best guesses, and instincts. Some of which don't always play out the way we expect.

Because the information we draw on may be only tangentially relevant to the current situation, these heuristic shortcuts give rise to cognitive biases.

We are all prone to cognitive bias. There are several dozen recognized forms of cognitive bias, some of which we have already looked at.

Here we focus on the few heuristics and biases most effective in persuading people to buy.

Scarcity

The scarcity heuristic leads us to value things that are less common over those that are more readily available.

We value things that are rare, expiring, selling out, or that are censored. In short, people want what they can't have.

You see this everywhere with collectors. Rare colours, rare coins, stamps, stores having closing-down sales, or end of range sales.

Even online stores use scarcity tactics, using "only xx remaining" in stock listings, or using countdown timers to create a sense of urgency.

People's fear of missing out (a combination of the pseudocertainty effect, which leads people to make riskier decisions to avoid a negative outcome than to achieve a positive one and reactance, which is the urge to do the opposite of what someone who you perceive to be controlling you or restricting your choice wants) will lead them to buy something they may not truly want, need, or have a use for, just to avoid wanting it later and it not being available.

I used to use this in timeshare sales all the time. I would say, "I'm not sure if it's still available, but one of our clients just upgraded his apartment, so we had an apartment I think would be great for you. If we still have it, would you buy this today?"

That showed that we sell the clients' apartments and upgrade them. It builds credibility and social proof at the same time. It also asks for a commitment to buy today, meaning I will get the deal if money is the only thing stopping him from buying, or get the objection if there is one.

All this while triggering the scarcity heuristic, which makes them want to buy it more.

Authority

If you are a professional in your field, people will listen to you more.

Would you listen to a fat, out of shape guy in the bar who told you not to go to the gym because it was bad for your heart? Would you listen if he told you to walk, but no more than twenty minutes a day, because it's counter-productive?

But if a doctor, with a couple of diplomas on his wall, told you the same thing, you would listen.

You would think there was something wrong with your heart, and you needed to take it easy, right?

You would assume the advice was specific to your medical condition, and not general bad advice.

That's authority at work, when it makes sense. We listen to the opinion of an authority figure, because we assume they know more about the subject than we do.

Authority becomes a bias, though, when we attribute more weight to the voice of an authority in one subject's opinion in an unrelated sphere, where they may not know as much as us, let alone more.

It's when we trust our doctor to give us financial advice, even though he may be in debt.

This tendency to extend positive evaluations of other's knowledge and attributes beyond their true extent is called the Halo Effect.

How do you create authority in sales? If possible, get someone to introduce you, and have them use a title, or something to build credibility.

For example, "Let me pass you over to John, he's our top salesman, he's been with us over ten years."

Or, "I'll introduce you to John, he's our resident expert on that."

This alone will increase sales.

Also, know your products, services, and industry, so that you can be a genuine authority and give sound advice.

Consistency

We all like to think of ourselves as being reasonable, intelligent, and consistent in our decision making.

So much so, that we have a bias blind spot, which leads us to believe other people are more biased than we are.

We also believe that our past decisions were better than they really were (choice-supportive bias).

We focus on and remember information that supports our beliefs (confirmation bias) and we forget that we may have held different opinions in the past (consistency bias.)

Add to this our tendency to imagine our future selves will have more willpower, make better decisions (present bias), and share our current beliefs and opinions (projection bias), and our tendency to overestimate the positive effects of a purchase on our mood and lifestyle, (impact bias) and you have a recipe for poor impulse control.

This is why so many adverts show aspirational images of people wearing designer clothes in fast cars, smiling families with perfect white teeth and flawless skin, and big expensive houses with pools and large gardens.

Because so many of our cognitive biases support our sense of hope for a positive future, if an ad (or a salesperson) can create an emotional response and trigger hope, our cognitive biases will do the rest.

In terms of consistency, though, our cognitive biases are just getting warmed up.

As if our inflated belief in our consistency wasn't enough, when we are consistent, it isn't always for the right reasons.

People are more inclined to make big commitments if they have made a series of smaller ones first.

They're also loathe to contradict anything they've already said for fear of looking foolish.

Strangely, and somewhat counterintuitively, people are more inclined to do another person a favour if they have already performed a favour for them in the past.

After all, if I ask you to pass me the salt you do, but when I ask you to pass the ketchup, you refuse for no apparent reason, you look unreasonable, right?

We call this the Ben Franklin Effect.

Con artists use this to get people to hand over personal details or large amounts of cash, by getting small details from you, or selling you smaller items first.

It's also why sales funnels and ladders work so well on the Internet, because your first purchase is a test purchase of low dollar value.

You get to decide for yourself if you like and trust the person before you invest large amounts in their training, software, or products and services.

So, it has advantages for both seller and customer, if used properly.

While this is understandable in terms of consistency what's really interesting is that people are more inclined to help someone they have previously done a favour for than someone who has previously done them a favour.

This has a variety of uses in sales.

If you get someone to write down their appointment time, they're much more likely to attend, even than if you write the appointment time on a card and give it to them.

Doctors and dentists have started requesting patients sign the register next to their appointment time and date, thereby creating a contract the patient is less likely to break and reducing wasted time in practices.

If you get a client to support you in some small way during the presentation, they are more likely to buy at the end.

Consensus

People do what other people do. Especially when they're in doubt. This is why social proof works so well.

The tendency to do or believe something because other people say or do it is called the Bandwagon Effect. The Availability Cascade also asserts that if something is repeated often enough, it becomes accepted as truth.

Thanks to the Continued Influence Effect, we also tend to stick to a belief once we have adopted it, even when presented with new evidence.

And while every parent knows how infuriating it can be to hear a teenager argue for the latest tech craze on the grounds that "everyone has one," or beg to go to a bar because "everyone does it," we never really grow out of peer pressure.

In timeshare, we used to use this by announcing people who just bought. We would even sometimes have a fake couple buy and applaud them to get the ball rolling.

Closing Objections

In sales, we talk about closes a lot. But what do we really mean?

We're talking about ways you control the conversation and influence the client or customer into making a buying decision.

This isn't mind control, manipulation, or taking advantage of people.

You shouldn't be selling anything you don't believe is a quality product at a reasonable price, and you shouldn't be selling anything to anyone who doesn't want, need, and have a use for something, or can't afford it.

But often people want to buy, they just need help justifying the decision to themselves. Sometimes they need a little push, and guidance to make the right choice.

There are several dozen established closing techniques you can learn and apply.

Different people often have different names for them, so don't get hung up on a label if I use a different label to the one you're used to.

Some closes suit different personalities better than others, too. So, you might try something and feel awkward or pushy saying it.

That's okay.

Practice a few times saying things to yourself in the mirror, changing the exact words and inflection until they come naturally to you.

If you still don't feel comfortable with a specific closing technique, don't use it.

Try another one. Experiment. Find the ones that work best for you that you're happy with and keep practicing until you do them so naturally you couldn't stop if you wanted to.

You don't have to know and use every close to be successful in sales.

Most people gravitate to a handful of closes and use them almost exclusively, because they work for them.

But knowing the other closes, for those times when the usual patter doesn't convince doesn't hurt, either.

The Alternative Close

The Alternative Close gives people a choice, but also assumes the purchase. It's a choice between two options, neither of which is a deal-breaker.

The Paperwork Close

The paperwork close allows you to take a step back from the salesperson's role into order taking. It's an assumptive close, because it sidesteps the decision, assuming it's a given.

You can use this throughout, from the opening to final closing.

You just ask, "Whose name will we be registering your new product in? Yours, or your spouse's?"

This includes an alternative close in there, but it can be used early on in a presentation to see if you are talking to the decision maker. It can also be used at the end and is a very powerful close.

The Delivery Close

A variant of the alternative close that assumes ownership is the delivery close.

"When would you like your package delivered, tomorrow morning, or tomorrow afternoon?"

It can be used at the end of a sale, combined with another close. You need to include, 'you' and 'yours.'

The "Think About What?" Close

If you're hearing, "I want to think about it," you need to find out what they need to think about.

A good way is to say, "Of course you want to think about it. I agree, you should think about it. What do you want to think about, the product, or the money?"

If it's the product, you can find out what it is they still aren't sure about and cover it for them, then move onto another close.

If it's the money, find out if it's the deposit or making instalments. If it's the deposit, find out if there's a way you can make it more manageable for them, using an, "If I could, would you?" close.

The 4 Questions Close

And another "Think About It" Close is the 4 Questions Close. You say, "Sure, do you want to think about it 2-3 days, or 2-3 weeks?"

Then, tell them, "Okay, most people's concerns can be answered by two or three questions. Is it okay if I share them with you, yes?"

This lowers their guard, because you're giving them time to think about it. Then you ask them:

"Do you like it?"

"Can you use it?"

"Do you understand it?"

"Can you afford it?"

If they say, "Yes," to all four, you can go back to a delivery or paperwork close.

The Missing Person Close

I have been using a "missing person" close in the call centre, when the decision maker isn't present, or they use a, "want to think about it," objection.

Here's what you say:

"Okay, I understand, I agree with you. I'll get this order through as agreed, and we'll add their name to the order, so they must sign for it. Is that fair enough?"

Or, "Okay, I understand, I agree. I'll get this order set up as agreed, subject only to their approval. Is that fair?"

That way you can get the contract made and get the paperwork done, and the decision maker only has to sign for it, which makes it a much easier decision for them to make.

Ideally, you would have somebody with the contracts when they are delivered who can close the missing person.

Another approach we use is, "Okay, does this person like what you have now?"

If they say, "Yes," you say, "Okay, so if what we're offering is more economical and/or offers more value, they would agree, yes?"

This highlights the fact they already have something they might be paying more for, or that isn't very different from what you're offering, and the other person already agreed to that. You can also combine that with putting the deal in their name, or subject to their approval.

The Understanding Close

Another way to approach this is to say, "Okay, I understand, and agree with you, but if your wife is anything like mine, she would never say, 'No,' to something that I love, and really want, and I wouldn't say 'No,' to her. So, whose name should I put it in, yours or your wife's?"

You need confidence to use this approach. It's a strong close, and it does work.

The "What If?" Close

Another great close I got from Grant Cardone works with the "I need to talk to..." objection. You ask, "What if they say 'No'?"

The most common answers to that are, "They won't say, 'No.' They never say, 'No,' to me if I want something."

In which case, you can do the paperwork close, and say, "Well, okay, so whose name shall I sign it in?" or the delivery close, "So, shall I send it tomorrow morning, or tomorrow night?"

If they say, "Then I wouldn't buy it," you ask, "What do you think they'll say 'No,' to, the product or the price?"

Once you know the objection, you can go back building value.

Either way, it's not a real objection. They're using the missing person as an excuse for something they are concerned with and want to think about.

It's a stalling tactic. If you approach it this way, you can still close them.

The Forgiveness Close

A Master Closer might say, "Okay, of course you have to talk to your wife. Let me asks you something. Do you like it? Can you use it? Do you want it? Do you understand it?"

If the answers are, "Yes," tell them, "Then it's better to ask forgiveness than permission."

This usually works. It tends to work better guy to guy or woman to woman, at least in my experience, but I would still use it on anyone.

The 1-10 Close

One of my favourite closes that I got from Grant Cardone is, "What would you rate our product on a scale from 1 to 10?"

If they give you a number less than 10, you ask, "Okay, what would make it a 10?"

If you do it this way, you can learn what they want and what their needs are and sell those to them. This is very effective combined with an, "If I could, would you?" close, and for upsells.

You can also use this with what they have already. If they have a product of your competitors' you ask them, "Okay, on a scale from 1 to 10, what would you give it?" Then you can show them how your product can meet those needs.

They may not be aware that their current provider may be able to meet those needs, and if you can show that you can, you can win the client.

You can also ask them to look back over the previous five similar purchases and rate those.

That puts your offering into perspective for them.

You can remind them, "But you still bought them."

Keep in mind, even if they rate the product a 7, and you can't increase that rating, people will still buy that product if it's what they need, and you can show them it's the best match available.

This close works great for people who have a product from a competitor that is cheaper than yours.

Because when they tell you, "I would like to have this, this, and that," provided you can meet those needs, you can use that to justify the price difference and add value to your offering.

Once you've explained the difference in terms of meeting their needs, they will understand and accept the higher price, because they are getting more out of it.

The "I agree" Close

I treat price objections as complaints, and simply agree, "Yes, it's expensive," or, "Yes, it's a lot of money."

Especially if it's a walk-in sale, where someone has walked into a store, or they have called you.

They already knew it was expensive. They came anyway. They will buy anyway.

Follow this up with an alternative close.

"I agree, it's expensive. Everyone who already bought it thought it was expensive. When do you want it delivered, tomorrow morning or tomorrow night?"

You could also say, "I agree. Be grateful you can do this for yourself and your family. I admire that. I hope I can do the same for my family one day." (if you don't already own the product.)

"So, would you like it in your name, or your spouse's?"

The Do It Anyway Close

Another way to handle price complaints, that I got from Grant Cardone, is to simply say, "I know it's a lot of money. Do it anyway."

"Do it anyway," is sometimes the only push they need. Everything they buy is expensive. People get over budget.

A spin off from that, which I train as a sympathetic close, is, "Do it for me. If you can't do it for you, and you can't do it for your family, do it for me."

That works very well, because it either gets the person laughing and doing it anyway if they have been sold well, or they say, "Are you crazy?

I'll do it for my family before I do it for you."

In which case, you go back to the delivery close.

"Okay, good, I understand. So, when do you want it delivered, tomorrow morning, or tomorrow afternoon?"

It's a combination of sympathetic and aggressive.

The Treat Yourself Close

When someone says, "It's too expensive," that can mean you haven't built the value enough.

But sometimes, you may have built the value in their mind, and they just can't justify it to themselves. Sometimes you just need to help them over that hurdle.

Say, "Of course it's expensive. Treat yourself, you deserve it."

You will be surprised how many people respond to that.

Take-Away Close

There are several Take-Away closes. These all use reverse psychology to sting the customer into action. Examples include:

"That's okay. I understand, you can't afford it. It's not for everyone."

"I'm not sure I can do that for you. It will take a lot of wheedling to set that up. I'm not going to do that for you unless you're committed to buying today. Do you want me to go ahead?"

"Tell you what, don't do it. Go home and think about it. And if when you come back, I don't have this deal, then take it as a sign it's not meant to be."

When you use a take-away, you then need to shut up and wait. This is a situation where, "he who speaks first, loses."

The Indecision Close

If someone tells you, "I can't make a decision today," tell them:

"Listen, either way, you're making a decision. You're either going to decide not to get what you want, or you're going to decide to get what you want. Either way, you're doing something, you're deciding. The question is, which decision will you make?"

I Want to Think About It

This objection comes up so much, it's worth giving it more attention and really making sure you know how to handle this.

How do you get a client who says they want to think about it to buy today?

First, understand that if you're hearing this, the presentation you gave was wrong for that customer.

This objection is best closed out early in the meeting, by getting the commitment to buy if you answer all their questions.

But if you didn't do that, and you confused them, how do you turn it around?

One way is to create urgency. Tell them there is a special offer today only.

Ask them, "Do you like it?" Because if they don't like it, there's no sale to be made.

If they like it, ask them, "Can you use it? Because even if you love it, if you can't use it, it's not for you."

If they can like it, and they can use it, ask, "Do

you understand it? Because if you don't understand it, I won't give you one. Because here we sell [your product experience] and I want to make sure you understand what you are buying."

If they like, can use, and understand the deal, ask, "Can you afford it? Because if you can't afford it, you can't have one. I'm sorry, I'm nice, but not that nice."

This not only is a take-away, which makes someone want the deal more, but it also pares the questions down to the basics and refocuses the buyer's attention.

In timeshare, we would end this refocus with, "If you like it, you can use it, you understand it, and you can afford it, we're going to ask you to buy it. I'm going to shake your hand. We're going to welcome you to the club, we're going to call Katerina to come here and give you your gift as we promised. Then we'll do the paperwork and escort you to the door. We'll thank you again, wish you a happy holiday, and tell you to come back and see us any time you like. Our door is always open.

"If you say, 'No,' that's okay. I will still shake your hand. I will still escort you to the door. I will still thank you for your time and give you your gift. That's okay. This isn't for everybody. We understand. The only thing I don't want to hear is stupid excuses like, 'I want to ask my mother, brother, sister, dog, or whoever. I don't want to hear 'I want to think about it.' Because we know these are all excuses. You know it. We know it. I'll give you an example…"

Then you tell a story. I'll give you the one I used to use, and you can customise it to suit yourself.

I Want to Think About It

I was walking in Oxford Street, in London, England. It was cold, and I saw this beautiful jacket in a shop window. So, I went inside.

I approached the assistant and asked her to try on the jacket. She said, "Of course,"reached it down, and walked towards me.

She held out the jacket, and I slid my arms inside it, and she lifted it up onto my shoulders.

It felt amazing.

It was beautiful.

The lining was silk, and sat flat, the jacked draped well. It was suede and leather, with textural interest, and it looked awesome. It was black. Deep black, rick and luxurious.

I loved it.

I looked in the mirror, and I looked ten times better, so I needed it.

I knew I could use it because it was cold outside.

I definitely understood what it would do for me.

So, I asked the price.

She said, "Of course, sir. Five thousand, four hundred pounds."

With a smile.

I slowly took the jacket off. I very slowly folded it, and gently put it back onto the counter.

I said, "Do you guys take credit card?"

She said, "Yes, of course we do, sir."

I said, "Okay. Do me a favour. Put the jacket aside. Don't let anything happen to that jacket. I want to think about it. I'll be back tomorrow."

Do you think I went back?

No, of course not, and neither will you. Because if you have to think about it with today's special offer, what's there to think about without it?

If you've primed them to think about financial logic correctly, it will work. Then you move into pricing them

Three Great Closes

You don't use a single close in isolation, at the end of your presentation. In practice, you'll develop your own style and adapt your favourite closing techniques in time.

Here, I want to give you an example of how closes can work together.

The Leading Close

I use two words a lot in my speech pattern when I speak. The first is, *yes*. The other is *now*.

I do this for two reasons.

First, instead of saying "Um," and "ah," as filler, because I give my presentations unrehearsed, I use words like "Now," at the start of a sentence, and end with "yes?"

These have the same effect of giving my brain time to process my thoughts and prepare the next words out of my mouth, without it sounding as though I'm scrabbling for words. They sound decisive and intentional, rather than reflexive and unthinking.

The second, more important reason, is that they lead the other person to agree with you, and to be prepared to act on your presentation.

For example, let's say I'm selling a car. And we're discussing speed, I might say something like, "Now, listen, I'm not saying you should go fast with this car, or that you should break the speed limit. But if you're in a tight spot or a situation, and you need to overtake someone, it's a lot safer, yes?"

"Now, it's nice to see you have that speed and that throttle when you need it, yes? See what I mean?"

Nine times out of ten, they will agree.

"Now, we all know iPhones have the least problems, yes?"

Find the things "everybody knows" about your product

Throughout your presentation, implement, "Yes, yes, yes," and "Now, now, now."

It's important to understand that it's not the words that matter so much as getting the client into a pattern of agreeing with you.

It doesn't matter if you say, "Yes?" "Right?" or "Okay?" So, relax, and use whatever comes naturally to you.

Nor is it important to get them to say the same words as you.

You might say, "You need a phone with a long battery life, right?"

They might be nodding, they might say, "Yes," "Uh-huh," or "That's right."

It's not the actual words that matter. It's the agreement. Don't get hung up on trying to force them to say specific words. You'll just come across as weird and controlling.

Now watch how this, used in combination with the other closes, can have a dramatic effect on your closing percentages.

Alternative Close

There are two ways to use alternative closes. The first way is to give a choice where you don't care what the answer is (because you can provide either option.) You just want to keep your customer making choices.

So, for example, if you're selling cars, you might ask, "Would you rather have a sports car and go faster, or an SUV that's easier going?"

Depending on the answer, you might say, "Ah, you want the sports car for the sexiness? Yes?" or "Ah, it's a lot safer, yes?"

Either way, you're both clarifying the answer, and reinforcing it. You're getting them to agree with you and building a pattern of yesses.

If you're selling holidays, you might ask, "Do you prefer a mountain view or a beach view?"

Then continue, "The mountain view because you're close to nature, there's less people, yes? Or the beach, because you can go fishing, go sunbathing, yes?"

You're giving them the benefits of both choices and getting them to make a decision that you have framed in a positive light.

By combining the alternative close with the leading language, you're guiding your customer into deciding, buying now, and saying yes. All these small leading techniques add up to an easier yes at the end of the presentation.

If you're trying to set appointments, or making sales phone calls, you use the alternative close a little differently.

You say, "I think you need to see this in person. When should I call, Thursday at six, or Friday at eight?"

By offering the choice like this, you have already taken it for granted they will see you, and you're just looking to set the time.

This avoids asking the client to set a time for an appointment and having them run through their schedule mentally and think of all the times they can't see you and why.

Instead, they're focused on which of the two days is better, and which of the two times is better. And if they have something scheduled at both of those times, they're more likely to come up with an alternative time on one of those two days.

What are you doing?

You're giving them a choice to make a decision.

Decision, decision, decision.

Now, now, now.

Three Great Closes

Yes, yes, yes.

You're building up a pattern.

You're raising the chances of them saying yes at the end of the presentation.

We used to use these techniques a lot in timeshare, where we had to have a same-day decision.

We used to sell off-site, before people even travelled to where we were selling. That meant we had to be convincing and get the sale the same day. There was no thinking about it or calling back later.

The alternative close also works on kids. "Do you want to do your homework now, or after supper?" They know they have to do their homework, but they feel they have a choice.

On a potential date. "Would you rather go for dinner or a movie?"

Even the heroes use it in movies, "We can do this the easy way or the hard way?"

If I could, would you?

You've done the presentation, and you're down to pricing. Hopefully, you're giving an alternative close at the end. Let's say that's cash or instalments. Either $4,000 cash, or $2,000 deposit and the rest in instalments.

You might say "Now, if you were going to buy from us today, would you prefer cash or instalments?"

This plays into the alternative close, but also bypasses the direct decision, by making the question theoretical "If you were to buy,"

But the answer assumes the customer is going to buy. Because if they weren't interested, they would tell you.

"Okay, so you prefer cash. Do we have a deal?"

If they say they have to think about it, you ask "What do you have to think about? Do you need to think about the deposit, or the instalments?"

If the answer is anything else, you have misjudged your presentation, but at least you can answer questions before coming back to the price issue.

Avoid this by always asking, "Other than the price, is there anything else that's stopping you from buying today?"

Get all those other objections out, and then deal with the price. At the end, the only thing the customer has to think about, if they have to think about it, should be the price.

If they say they have to think about the price, you might say, "Take a few moments to think about it, I'll be right back."

Time share is very aggressive in sales techniques. I was an aggressive salesperson, and there was no coming back, because of the setup. It wasn't an option.

So, we would have a twenty percent discount for buying on the day. And there are ways to make customers believe they can't get the same price any other day.

So, circling back to the question. "What do you have to think about, the deposit, or instalments?"

If it's the deposit, you say, "Too expensive, yes? If I could lower the deposit and transfer it to the instalments, would you buy today?"

Or a customer might say they can't pay the deposit today. You might ask, "When can you pay the deposit?"

Whatever the answer, you say, "I don't know if I can do this, it's a big stretch. But if I ask my director/manager if you could pay the deposit then, would you buy it today? Yes?"

That's the close. If I could change this one aspect of the deal to match your requirements, would you buy from me today?

Most of the time, there's some leeway. You might not even need to ask your boss. But you should anyway, for two reasons.

One, to double-check you're not giving going to hit after-sales issues with any concessions.

Also because if you said you needed permission, and then made the change without checking, you look untrustworthy in your customers' eyes.

Referrals

You need to get referrals whether you are selling on the phone, online, or in person.

It's easier to approach someone and say, "Hi, I'm Paul. Your friend Max gave me your details because he just joined our family, and he thinks we would be a great fit for you" than, "Hi, My name is Paul, I'm calling from…"

It's much easier to break the ice, and it's not cold calling any more, it's making a connection based on a mutual acquaintance's suggestion. This is particularly useful in B2B sales.

When you're selling to consumers, you may need to get the customer to make the introduction for you.

But how do you get referrals?

The easiest way to get referrals is right after a completed sale, ask, "Real quick, think of two names who could benefit from this."

This is more effective than asking, "Do you know anyone who would like this?" because it gives them a specific number to focus on, and it isn't overwhelming.

But don't just get the names. You need to get the numbers, and the introduction.

This is easier in business, so let's look at that first.

If you're selling B2B, your customer might be able to give you the names and positions of referrals, and that might be all you need to make the contact.

But if you can, get them to call their contacts and introduce you. Just ask them to say, "I'm with Paul at SellAPen Sales Training, and I think you need to sit down with this guy and see what he can do for you. Let me put him on now so you can set something up."

Then quickly set an appointment and get off the phone.

If they won't make a call, ask them to send an email or text right then to their contacts, telling them to expect your call. Anything that comes from the contact rather than you helps when you make that first call.

With consumer sales, you can't ask customers to give out other people's contact details without breaching their privacy.

But you can't just rely on customers to remember to tell their friends about you and recommend you. I usually ask them to make the call on the spot as they are happy with their purchase.

If you can, offer some kind of referral incentive. If you offer a subscription service, it might be a free month for each of them if they refer a friend. Or a free upgrade.

If you sell products, you might offer a small cashback incentive to existing customers who recommend new ones. But if you do that, make sure the new customer receives the same reward.

Incentives where only the existing customer is rewarded for bringing in new business turn your customers into affiliates.

That reduces the value of their endorsement of you in their friends' eyes and can backfire.

Putting it all together

Now let's put all of that together, and imagine you've just been asked the dreaded question:

"Sell me this pen."

What's the first thing you're going to do?

Put the pen away. Put it in your pocket. Forget about the pen for a minute.

Smile.

Introduce yourself.

Then start asking questions.

You might ask:

"Okay, so how long have you been in the market for a pen?" or, "How long have you been looking for a pen?"

The customer might say, "Three months," he might say "two months," he might say "one month," he might say, "I'm not looking for a pen."

But you have to start asking questions. And ask several questions, to establish interest.

How to Sell a Pen Really

Assuming the interviewer is playing nice, and says they are looking for a pen, what kind of pen were they looking for?

A black pen?

A thick pen?

A small pen?

What would they want to use the pen for?

Once you have established interest, you need to find the needs of your customer.

For example, I use a Mont Blanc. I use it for signing contracts, and for when I do meetings, so I can pull out a nice pen.

But let's take this a step further. Ask questions like, "What do you usually use a pen for?"

"When do you use a pen?"

"When was the last time you used a pen?"

"What do you like about your current pen?"

"What do you wish you could change about your current pen?"

These questions will tell you a lot about your client.

Maybe they are a salesperson that just signed a deal. Maybe they're a traffic warden writing tickets on the road.

You ask questions for two reasons.

The first is for you; to get information and find

Putting It All Together

out the needs of your customer.

But also, it's for your customer to understand and find out why he needs a pen. Because until then, he might not see the need for one.

You have to create need. People don't know they want something or need something until it's brought to their attention, and they understand why they need it.

So, once you have established the need for a pen, you're going to reintroduce your pen.

Take it out of your pocket, tell them, "Based on what you've told me today, I think this is the pen you're looking for."

Then feed back to them what they've told you and relate that to your pen.

Then hand it to them, and ask them to sign their name, to give it a try.

Now an interviewer is likely to start throwing objections at you and asking questions.

If somebody he asks you a question, for example, "What colour does the pen write?" Never answer, "Black," or "Red."

The answer is always, "What colour would you want it to write?" (Or, "It's available in black, red, or blue, which would you prefer?")

If they ask you, "Is that a black pen?"

The answer is, "Would you like it to be a black pen?"

Let me explain.

The reason you do not want to give a straight answer is because you don't want to block the sale.

Let's say you ask me, "Is it a black pen?" and I say, "Yes," then you say, "Too bad I really need a red pen," at that point, I closed myself out. The sale is lost.

If you ask me if it's a ballpoint, and I say, "Yes," then when you say, "I only write with fountain pens," again the sale is lost.

This is especially true if you don't have another pen to sell.

Even if you do, and say, "Oh, but I have a red one," then you're trying to push. And even worse, you're trying to sell something that's perceived as second best, because you didn't offer it first.

So, you never answer directly.

The correct answer is, "Would you like it to be a ball-point?"

"Would you prefer a black pen?"

Never answer, always ask them if that's what they want. That way, if it's a yes, you can continue without pushing the product.

You might hype the pen or keep answering questions until the interviewer runs out of objections.

But remember, you're not being asked to show your knowledge of how to answer objections, you're being asked to sell the pen.

So, at some point you have to ask for the sale.

It doesn't really matter how you do it, it matters when.

As soon as you hear buying signals, just ask, "So would you like me to wrap that up for you?" or "Would you like it in a presentation box, or in your pocket?"

If you get more objections, the next time you get a buying signal, say, "It sounds to me as though you like it. So, other than price, is there anything else stopping you buying this pen from me today?"

Then you'll either get more objections to answer, after which you can repeat the question until you get a "no."

Then, as it's an interview, and it's a trick question anyway, borrow a trick from Zig Ziglar.

When put on the spot by Johnny Carson and asked to sell him an ashtray, he first asked why Carson would want it.

When Carson replied, it looked like a well-made, good ashtray, Ziglar then said, "'Okay, but you'd have to tell me what you think it's worth to you."

When Carson replied $20 seemed about right, Ziglar simply said, "Sold."

So, when the interviewer gives you a price, shake his hand.

Now, Sell Me A Pen

Remember at the start of the book I told you there was a competition to enter once you'd read it?

Now you have, here it is

The Sell A Pen.com
Salesmanship Awards

I want you to sell me a pen, in a video.

In brief.

Record your best pitch, trying to sell me your pen. It can be any pen you like.

Post your video on YouTube with the phrase *SellAPen.com Awards Entry* in the title.

Include the phrase, "This is my SellAPen,com Salesmanship Awards entry for ..." (with the current month and year) in the video description.

Go to the YouTube.com/PaulDemocritou and find

the Sell A Pen Awards Playlist. Watch the first video, introducing the competition.

Post a comment under the video with a link to your video entry.

Remember to watch and vote for your favourite videos and share the competition page on your social media accounts.

Winners will be chosen based on merit by myself and guest judges that may include Ben Gay III, Sandra Gail Seymour, and others who may be invited to participate in the judging from time to time.

Prizes available include books, training courses, telephone consultations, and sales training materials.

You can find full rules and resources and enter the competition at http://SellAPen.com.

About the Author

Paul Democritou is an entrepreneur, sales and marketing expert, author, and a blockchain / ICO advisor. He is also known as an entertainer and director and was responsible for over 15 VMA's and 2 EMA nominations as a video producer.

As a very successful sales and marketing expert in the timeshare industry which later expanded to other fields and companies, Paul provides online and offline training to companies and individuals.

In 2016, Paul was diagnosed with Non-Hodgkin's Lymphoma – cancer. He wrote the book *SUCCESS!* that was born as a result of vision and passion to help others succeed even in harsh conditions.

Paul also recently wrote *The Closers - Part 3* with living legend Ben Gay III. He is currently advising ICO's in the block-chain industry, while working on his upcoming books.

Connect at PaulDemocritou.com

Also by Paul Democritou

SUCCESS!

Improvise, Adapt, Overcome

Success isn't easy. The dreams modern media sell you should come with a warning: You need to know how to think to succeed. You also need money to make money and wishing the universe would give it to you without taking action is... a little farfetched!

Success! Improvise, Adapt, Overcome is the only book to include action plans so you start making money in any situation you're in, even with zero capital.

While there's no such thing as guaranteed success, there are established principles, and breadcrumbs you can follow. Paul Democritou lays out a path that anyone can follow to become successful - no matter what life has thrown at you so far. By learning to Improvise, Adapt, and Overcome, and following his 11-step action plan, you can change your mindset, and upgrade your life, however hopeless it might seem.

Get Your Copy Now at TheClosers3.com

Get Your Copy Now at TheClosers3.com

Bibliography

Bregman, P. (2015, May 26). *If You Want People To Listen, Stop Talking*. Retrieved from Psychology Today: https://www.psychologytoday.com/us/blog/how-we-work/201505/if-you-want-people-listen-stop-talking

King, J. (n.d.). *Why "Practice Makes Perfect"*. Retrieved from Centre for Motivation and Change: https://motivationandchange.com/why-practice-makes-perfect/

Kruger, J., & Dunning, D. (Dec 1999). Unskilled and unaware of it: How difficulties in recognizing one's own incompetence lead to inflated self-assessments. *Journal of Personality and Social Psychology*, 1121-1134.

NBC News. (2017, November 28). *Smiling can trick your brain into happiness — and boost your health*. Retrieved from NBC News Better: https://www.nbcnews.com/better/health/smiling-can-trick-your-brain-happiness-boost-your-health-ncna822591

The power of temptation. (2009, 08 03). Retrieved from Northwestern Kellog: https://www.kellogg.northwestern.edu/news_articles/2009/nordgren_research.aspx

Tsu, S. (n.d.). *The Art of War*.

www.ingramcontent.com/pod-product-compliance
Lightning Source LLC
Chambersburg PA
CBHW020435220526
45464CB00002B/713